Pebble® Plus

BIG
BIG ROLLER COASTERS

by Catherine Ipcizade

Consulting Editor: Gail Saunders-Smith, PhD

Consultant: Mark Cole, President
American Coaster Enthusiasts

Capstone press®

Mankato, Minnesota

Pebble Plus is published by Capstone Press,
151 Good Counsel Drive, P.O. Box 669, Mankato, Minnesota 56002.
www.capstonepress.com

Books published by Capstone Press are manufactured with paper
containing at least 10 percent post-consumer waste.

Library of Congress Cataloging-in-Publication Data
Ipcizade, Catherine.
    Big roller coasters / by Catherine Ipcizade.
    p. cm. — (Pebble plus. Big)
    Includes bibliographical references and index.
    Summary: "Simple text and photographs present big roller coasters" — Provided by publisher.
    ISBN 978-1-4296-3315-4 (library binding)
1. Roller coasters — Juvenile literature. I. Title. II. Series.
GV1860.R64I63 2010
791.06'8 — dc22   2009001616

Editorial Credits
Erika L. Shores, editor; Ted Williams, designer; Jo Miller, media researcher

Photo Credits
Alamy/Jim Lane, 13; Malaysia Collection/Hornbil Images, 15; Sinibomb Images, 7
Corbis/Kevin Fleming, 19
Newscom/AFP/Kazuhiro Nogi, 21
Shutterstock/Cary Kalscheuer, 5; javarman, cover (background); John Leung, 1; Lim Yong Hian, cover (tracks);
    Stavchansky Yakov, cover; Xavier Pironet, 17
SuperStock, Inc./age footstock, 11
Wikimedia/WillMcC/GNU Free Documentation License, 9

Note to Parents and Teachers

The Big set supports national science standards related to technology. This book describes and
illustrates big roller coasters. The images support early readers in understanding the text. The
repetition of words and phrases helps early readers learn new words. This book also introduces
early readers to subject-specific vocabulary words, which are defined in the Glossary section.
Early readers may need assistance to read some words and to use the Table of Contents,
Glossary, Read More, Internet Sites, and Index sections of the book.

Table of Contents

Big

Roller coasters give
riders big thrills.
Coasters zoom around
loops and race down hills.

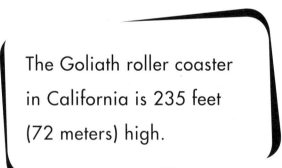

The Goliath roller coaster
in California is 235 feet
(72 meters) high.

Single-car coasters race

on big tracks alone.

No cars pull or push.

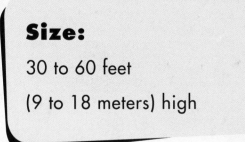

Size:
30 to 60 feet
(9 to 18 meters) high

Bobsled coasters glide
down big slides.
Walls keep cars safe.

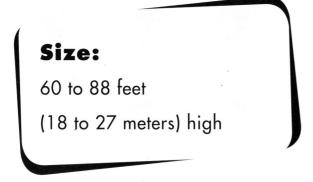

Size:
60 to 88 feet
(18 to 27 meters) high

Riders zoom through the air
on a flying roller coaster.
Seats hang from big tracks.

Size:

50 to 170 feet
(15 to 52 meters) high

Biggest

Harnesses go over
riders' shoulders
on inverted coasters.
Big loops turn riders
upside down.

Size:
149 to 215 feet
(45 to 66 meters) high

Big wooden planks crisscross
under cars on wooden coasters.
Riders speed down a 155-foot
(47-meter) drop on the
Mean Streak wooden coaster.

Size:
25 to 218 feet
(8 to 66 meters) high

Seats spin in all directions on a 4th Dimension coaster. This wild coaster sends riders headfirst down big hills.

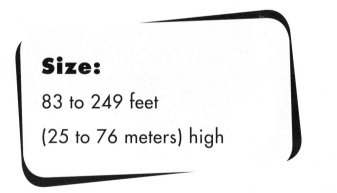

Size:
83 to 249 feet
(25 to 76 meters) high

Glossary

conductor — a person who drives a train

harness — a set of straps or bars that hold a rider safely in place on a roller coaster

inverted — upside down

loop — a circle

plank — a piece of wood that holds something in place

thrill — a feeling of excitement

track — a set of steel or wooden rails that make a path for roller coasters and trains

Read More

Mason, Paul. *Roller Coaster!* Chicago: Raintree, 2007.

Stone, Lynn M. *Roller Coasters.* How Are They Built? Vero Beach, Fla.: Rourke, 2002.

Internet Sites

FactHound offers a safe, fun way to find Internet sites related to this book. All of the sites on FactHound have been researched by our staff.

Here's all you do:

Visit *www.facthound.com*

FactHound will fetch the best sites for you!

Index

Word Count: 142
Grade: 1
Early-Intervention Level: 21

Bigger

A conductor doesn't drive
this big train.
Twisting turns make
train roller coasters wild rides.

Size:
25 to 100 feet
(8 to 30 meters) high

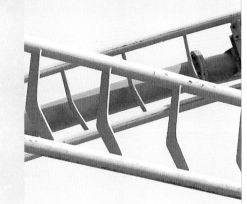

Riders don't sit on standing roller coasters. The Chang standing coaster has a big 144-foot (44-meter) drop.

Size:
90 to 156 feet
(27 to 47 meters) high